Swap Day

Written by Lisa Thompson
Pictures by Luke Jurevicius and Arthur Moody

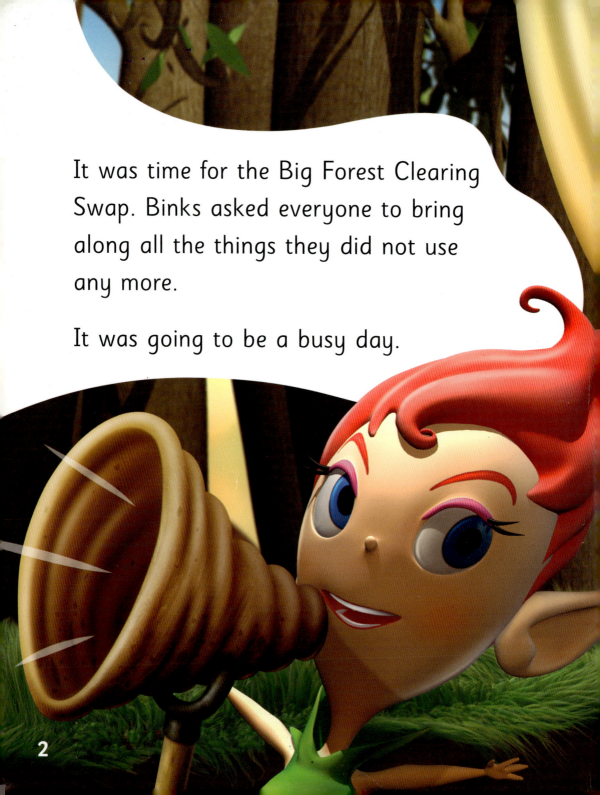

It was time for the Big Forest Clearing Swap. Binks asked everyone to bring along all the things they did not use any more.

It was going to be a busy day.

Everyone met at the clearing, which was a part of the forest where there was a big gap in the trees. They all had things to swap.

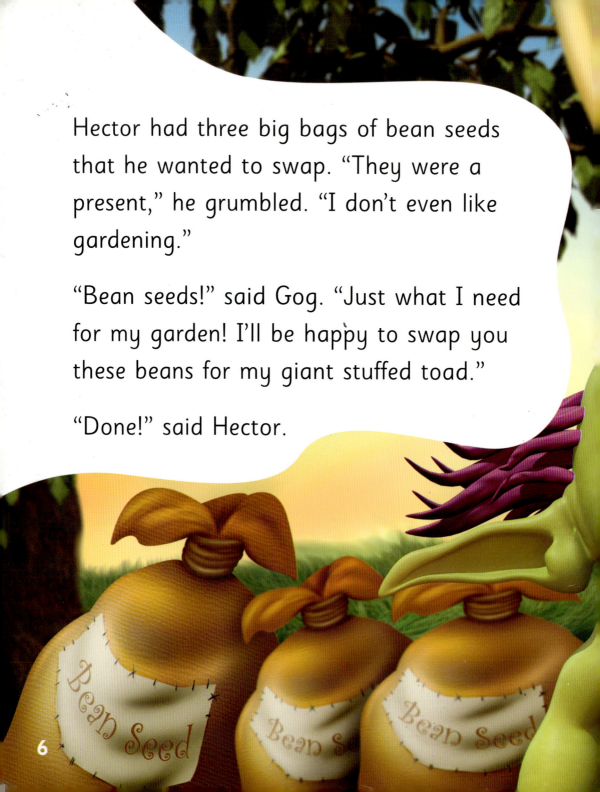

Hector had three big bags of bean seeds that he wanted to swap. "They were a present," he grumbled. "I don't even like gardening."

"Bean seeds!" said Gog. "Just what I need for my garden! I'll be happy to swap you these beans for my giant stuffed toad."

"Done!" said Hector.

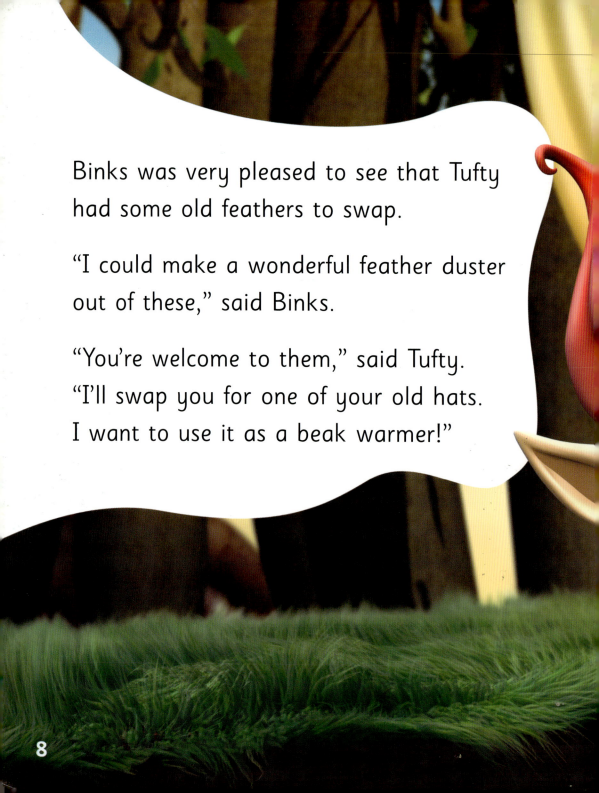

Binks was very pleased to see that Tufty had some old feathers to swap.

"I could make a wonderful feather duster out of these," said Binks.

"You're welcome to them," said Tufty. "I'll swap you for one of your old hats. I want to use it as a beak warmer!"

Dash had two old unicorn shoes that she wanted to swap.

Nuggle was thrilled. "I'll take those!" she said. "Unicorn shoes are lucky. I could spin a very lucky web between your old shoes!"

Nuggle gave Dash some extra strong spider thread in return for the shoes.

Boo wanted Hector's jar of river slime. "That slime looks wonderful!" said Boo. "Really nasty!"

"Yes," said Hector. "It's very scary stuff!"

"Great!" said Boo. "I'll give you my old screeching ball for it."

"Is that all? Well... OK," grumbled Hector.

Big Eyes had some old books he no longer wanted. They were large and dusty.

Binks cleaned off the dust.

"How wonderful!" she said. "These are all stories about elves! I can read them, and then use them to stand on so that I can reach high shelves."

Binks gave Big Eyes an old pair of glasses in return for the books.

Gog found a colourful hat that went with the glasses. Big Eyes put them on.

"Wow!" he said. "I look really cool!"

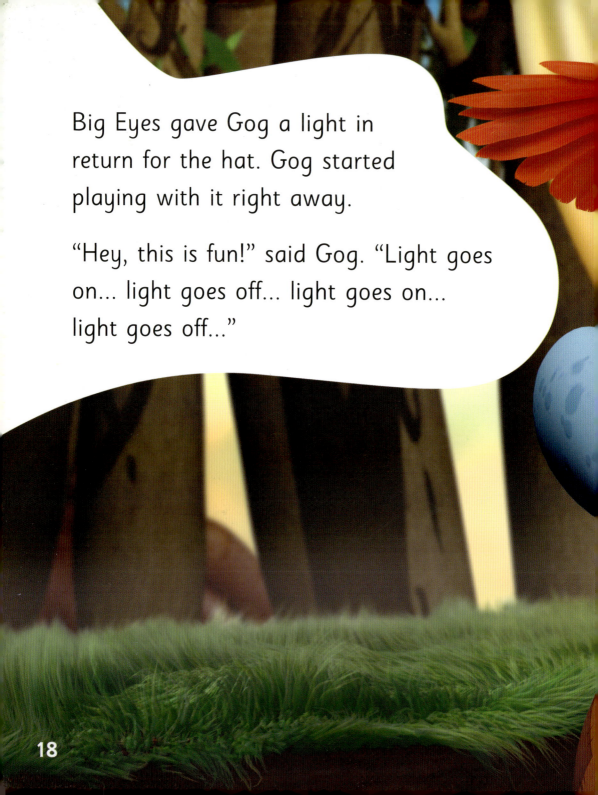

Big Eyes gave Gog a light in return for the hat. Gog started playing with it right away.

"Hey, this is fun!" said Gog. "Light goes on... light goes off... light goes on... light goes off..."

Everyone was having lots of fun swapping things. Even Hector stopped being grumpy for a while. He loved his screeching ball and his giant stuffed toad. He even went away with some toy farm animals.

"I never knew I wanted these!" he said.

At the end of the day, no one had any of the things they started off with.

But they all had just as much stuff to take home!